Diversified Streams: Mastering Multiple Sources of Income in 2023

Chapter 1:The Power of Income Diversification

Chapter 2: Shaping the Modern Economy

Chapter 3: The Gig Economy: A Door to Multiple Incomes

Chapter 4: Passive Income: Money While You Sleep

Chapter 5: The Digital Gold Rush: Exploring Online Entrepreneurship

Chapter 6: Side Businesses: Turning Passion into Profit

Chapter 7: Real Estate Investments: Building Wealth, One Property at a Time

Chapter 8: Peer-to-Peer Lending: The Rise of Social Finance

Chapter 9: Navigating Challenges and Risks: The Realities of Multiple Income Streams

Chapter 10: The Dawn of a New Era: Future Trends in Income Generation

Conclusion: The End of a Chapter, The Start of a Journey

Table of Contents

Chapter 1: The Power of Income Diversification

Income diversification is not a new concept. As long as money has been around, people have been finding various ways to earn it. However, the landscape of income generation has changed dramatically in recent years. With the rise of the digital age, the gig economy, and technological advancements, multiple streams of income have become more accessible and crucial than ever before.

Chapter 2: Shaping the Modern Economy

In the past, the traditional path was clear: finish school, land a good job, work for years, and retire with a decent pension. Today, this path is less defined. Economic instability, job insecurity, and an increase in flexible work options have reshaped how we perceive income. This chapter will guide you through the realities of the modern economy and why you need to consider having multiple income sources.

Chapter 3: The Gig Economy: A Door to Multiple Incomes

The gig economy is an increasingly important part of the global economy, and it provides an accessible door to income diversification. We will explore various gig economy options, ranging from freelance writing and design work to rideshare driving and property rentals.

Chapter 4: Passive Income: Money While You Sleep

Imagine making money while you're sleeping, on vacation, or while doing your favorite hobbies. This isn't a dream – it's the power of passive income. This chapter will discuss various types of passive income, including investing in stocks, real estate rentals, royalties from books or music, and more.

Chapter 5: Making Money Online: From E-commerce to Content Creation

The Internet has made earning money more accessible than ever before. Whether you're interested in selling products through an online store, creating engaging content on social platforms, or offering your skills as a remote freelancer, this chapter will guide you through the myriad of online income opportunities.

Chapter 6: Building a Side Business

A side business can be an excellent source of additional income and can even become a full-time endeavor. From idea generation to business planning and marketing strategies, this chapter will provide a comprehensive guide to starting and running a successful side business.

Chapter 7: Investing for Income

Investing can seem daunting, but it's a critical part of securing future financial freedom and creating another income stream. In this chapter, we'll simplify the world of investing, covering stocks, bonds, mutual funds, real estate, and the rising world of cryptocurrency.

Chapter 8: Strategies for Success

Having multiple income streams is not just about making more money; it's about financial security, independence, and freedom. But success doesn't come without strategies. This chapter will outline key tactics to effectively manage and maximize your income streams.

Chapter 9: Navigating Challenges and Risks

Every income source has its own set of challenges and risks. Recognizing these potential pitfalls can prepare you for any hurdles and help ensure your multiple income streams' longevity and profitability.

Chapter 10: The Dawn of a New Era: Future Trends in Income Generation

The chapter also examines the transformative impacts of automation and artificial intelligence, suggesting that rather than replacing jobs, these technologies are creating new income-generating opportunities. Another major trend highlighted is the increasing emphasis on sustainable and socially responsible investing, where investors seek not just financial returns, but also positive environmental and social impacts.

"Diversified Streams: Mastering Multiple Sources of Income in 2023" is your comprehensive guide to navigating, creating, and managing multiple income sources in the modern world. The path to financial freedom isn't linear – it's a diverse and winding road. But with this book as your guide, you'll be well-equipped to traverse it confidently.

Chapter 1

The Power of Income Diversification

In a rapidly changing world where economic and job market stability is more volatile than ever, the wisdom of depending solely on a single source of income seems less applicable. The concept of income diversification is a method to safeguard against financial unpredictability and hardship. Simply put, to diversify your income is to create multiple streams from which money flows into your life, thereby increasing your financial security and potential for wealth accumulation.

This concept is no stranger to the world of finance, echoing the practice of investment diversification. It's a simple yet powerful maxim: "Don't put all your eggs in one basket." In the realm of income, this strategy involves cultivating several independent or semi-independent revenue streams. This way, if one source faces a downturn – perhaps due to economic fluctuations, industry disruption, or personal circumstances – the impact on your overall income is softened.

But beyond being a safety net, income diversification also opens up opportunities for increased wealth. When you establish multiple sources of income, you're not just creating a fallback - you're also multiplying your revenue. Each stream can contribute to your financial pot, and as they grow, so too does your overall income. This process can potentially expedite your journey towards financial freedom and even early retirement.

Moreover, diversification doesn't have to be a chore or a dry financial tactic. It can be an exciting exploration of passion projects and interests. For instance, if you're passionate about photography, why not start selling prints online or offer freelance photography services? Love writing? Consider starting a blog and monetizing it through advertising, sponsored content, or subscription fees. Diversifying income can not only supplement your main income but also provide a creative outlet and an opportunity to capitalize on your talents.

However, embarking on the journey towards income diversification is not without its challenges. It requires research, planning, commitment, and sometimes an initial investment. Yet the potential benefits – financial security, wealth growth, and the freedom to explore passions – make it a worthwhile endeavor.

Throughout the following chapters, we will delve into different avenues for diversifying income, discussing their benefits, challenges, and strategies for success. We'll cover everything from the gig economy and online entrepreneurship to investments and passive income strategies. Whether you're an employee looking to supplement your wages, a retiree seeking extra retirement income, or an entrepreneur aiming to expand your business revenue, this guide aims to equip you with the knowledge and inspiration to navigate and master the world of income diversification in 2023.

Chapter 2

Shaping the Modern Economy

There was a time when life's roadmap was crystal clear, almost comfortably predictable. You'd finish school, find a decent job, plant yourself there and cultivate a career, a legacy. The promise of a 'job for life' wasn't an alien concept. With hard work and dedication, you'd climb the corporate ladder and, eventually, retire with a golden handshake, a nice pension to look forward to. It was a path trodden by our parents and grandparents, a tried and true narrative etched in our societal fabric.

But today? The world we navigate is vastly different, and the old roadmap seems less applicable in the face of an evolving economy. Our economic landscape has transformed beyond recognition, with technological advancements, global events, and paradigm shifts in workforce trends playing the lead roles.

In this modern era, no job comes with a lifetime guarantee. We've witnessed the rise and fall of industry giants, once considered invincible, toppled by unforeseen disruptions. The harsh reality? The rug can be pulled out from under our feet at any moment, leaving those who rely on a single income source vulnerable.

Yet, while job security may be a fading concept, the dawn of this new era also brought an unprecedented level of flexibility and potential for entrepreneurship. We've seen the office walls crumble as remote work and digital nomadism rise, allowing us to trade stuffy cubicles for cozy home offices or sun-soaked beachside cafes. Traditional 9-to-5 roles are giving way to freelance and gig work, untethering us from rigid schedules and offering control over our own time.

However, it's not all rosy. Modern living, particularly in the city, comes with a hefty price tag. Soaring living costs often outpace wage growth, forcing us to stretch our paychecks to the limit. This financial strain necessitates additional income sources, not just to meet ends, but to build a cushion for the future.

It's a lot to take in, this modern economy of ours. Yes, it comes with its fair share of challenges and uncertainties. But it also presents a golden opportunity for those willing to adapt and seize the potential of multiple income streams. From the gig economy and online entrepreneurship to remote work and side businesses, there's a vast ocean of opportunities waiting to be explored.

In the upcoming chapters, we'll take a deep dive into these opportunities. We'll learn to navigate the ebb and flow of the gig economy, tap into the wealth of online entrepreneurship, and master the art of balancing a side business. We'll decode the mysteries of creating and managing multiple income streams, building not just a safety net, but a launchpad for financial growth and independence. Here's to embracing the challenges of our modern economy and turning them into opportunities for financial prosperity.

Chapter 3

The Gig Economy: A Door to Multiple Incomes

Think back to a time when the job market was a rigid construct, made up of traditional roles, fixed hours, and long-term contracts. You signed on the dotted line, and your life was suddenly committed to an organization, your daily routine set in stone. But those times are changing. The rise of the gig economy has transformed how we view work, income, and career progression.

The term "gig economy" refers to a labor market characterized by the prevalence of short-term contracts or freelance work as opposed to permanent jobs. It's an economy where the worker is less of an employee and more of an independent contractor, offering their skills to businesses and individuals on a project-by-project basis. In essence, the gig economy champions flexibility and individual control over work, a stark contrast to the fixed and rigid structure of traditional employment.

Participating in the gig economy can be as simple as signing up for a platform like Uber or Lyft to become a driver in your spare time. Or, it might mean offering your skills as a freelance graphic designer, writer, or programmer on websites such as Upwork or Fiverr. It can even include renting out that spare room in your house via Airbnb. The possibilities are plentiful, each presenting a unique opportunity to generate income.

But what truly sets the gig economy apart is its accessibility and flexibility. For one, it offers a platform to those who may struggle to find work in a traditional job market, such as students, stay-at-home parents, or retirees. It also provides an opportunity to turn a passion or a hobby into a source of income. Perhaps you love designing websites, baking unique pastries, or providing guided tours of your city. The gig economy opens a door for these talents to earn you some extra cash.

Moreover, the gig economy allows for control over your work-life balance. Since you dictate the terms of your work – when, where, and how much you work – it's possible to mold your gig work around your life, not the other way around.

However, while the gig economy offers numerous benefits, it's not without its challenges. Job security, inconsistent income, and a lack of traditional benefits like health care and retirement plans are common concerns for gig workers. It requires careful planning and financial management to create a sustainable income stream within the gig economy.

Over the coming chapters, we'll examine these challenges more in-depth and explore strategies to overcome them - giving you a full grasp of how you can navigate the gig economy successfully.

Chapter 4

Passive Income: Money While You Sleep

Have you ever dreamt of earning money while sipping a cup of coffee at a Parisian cafe, hiking in the Rocky Mountains, or simply curling up with a good book at home? It might sound like a fantasy, but it's more achievable than you might think, thanks to the concept of passive income.

Passive income refers to earnings derived from a source that requires little to no effort to maintain. It's the notion of "making money while you sleep," creating a revenue stream that works independently of your active involvement. Sounds dreamy, right? However, it's important to note that most passive income sources require significant initial effort, investment, or both. But once they're set up and running, they can provide a consistent and, in some cases, substantial income stream.

So, what are these magical sources of passive income?

One of the most common and accessible ways is through investing. This can be in the form of dividend-paying stocks, bonds, mutual funds, or real estate. Here, your money works for you, earning interest, dividends, or rental income without requiring your constant attention.

Another popular method is through digital products or online businesses. For example, you could write and sell an e-book, create an online course, or develop a mobile app. While these require initial effort to create and market, once they're out in the digital world, they can generate revenue without constant work.

Affiliate marketing is another avenue. Here, you promote a product or service on your website or social media platform and receive a commission for every sale made through your referral link.

Royalties from creative work shouldn't be overlooked either; musicians, writers and artists who produce creative work may see royalties from it come rolling in long after creation has taken place. Every book sold, every song downloaded or piece licensed could become another source of passive income for you.

But remember, passive income isn't all sunshine and rainbows. It often requires significant upfront investment, either in the form of time, money, or both. There's also the challenge of market competition, especially in online ventures. And don't forget about the tax implications of passive income, which can be different from regular income.

In the following chapters, we will break down these passive income streams in more detail, exploring the opportunities, challenges, and strategies for success. With the right approach, passive income can serve as a powerful tool in your multiple income streams arsenal, offering financial growth, stability, and yes, the chance to make money while you sleep.

Chapter 5

The Digital Gold Rush: Exploring Online Entrepreneurship

Once upon a time, striking gold meant venturing into the wild, armed with a pickaxe, a pan, and a lot of hope. Today, we're in the midst of a different kind of gold rush – a digital one. And our tools? A good internet connection, a laptop, and a dose of creativity and determination.

Welcome to the world of online entrepreneurship.

Just as the internet has infiltrated every corner of our lives – changing how we communicate, learn, shop, and even date – it's revolutionized the face of entrepreneurship. Gone are the days when starting a business meant hefty loans, physical premises, and a local-only reach. Today, all you need is a digital platform and a great idea to reach a global audience.

E-commerce is the modern marketplace. If you've got something to sell, the world is your customer. It might be your grandmother's secret apple pie recipe, vintage clothes you've collected over the years, or digital assets like graphic designs or e-books. Platforms like Amazon, eBay, Shopify, and WooCommerce have made it easier than ever to set up your virtual shop front.

If you're more of a storyteller, consider the world of blogging, vlogging, or podcasting. Do you have travel tales that could fill a book? Or perhaps you're a DIY guru, ready to share your home improvement hacks with the world? With engaging content and a flair for creativity, you can gather a virtual crowd ready to hang on your every word. Monetization comes in many forms – advertising, sponsorships, or even fan donations via platforms like Patreon.

Affiliate marketing is another trail to consider. Here, you become the trusted middleman, recommending products or services and earning a commission for each customer you lead to a sale.

And for the tech wizards, the digital realm is your playground. Whether it's developing a life-changing app, a game that's the next Angry Birds, or handy software solutions, your creations can command significant income.

But let's not sugarcoat it – just like the original gold rush, striking it rich isn't guaranteed. The internet, while filled with opportunities, is a crowded space. Making your mark and building a reputable online presence takes time, patience, and a lot of hard work. Technical glitches, website crashes, even cyber threats – they're all par for the course.

But don't let that discourage you. In the chapters ahead, we'll delve deeper into the minefield of online entrepreneurship. We'll explore the ups and downs, the twists and turns, and provide you with a map to navigate it all. So grab your digital pickaxe and let's venture forth into the world of online entrepreneurship. Your gold nugget could be just a click away.

Chapter 6

Side Businesses: Turning Passion into Profit

In the hustle and bustle of our daily lives, we often have passions, hobbies, or talents that take a back seat. Perhaps you love to paint, craft artisanal candles, or have a knack for dog training. Maybe you've discovered an unmet need in your local community, and you've thought, "I wish someone would do something about that." Well, that someone could be you. Welcome to the world of side businesses.

A side business is a venture you start and run in addition to your regular job. It's a way of earning extra income, but it's also more than that. It's an opportunity to explore your passions, utilize your skills, and perhaps even make a positive impact in your community.

A common form of a side business is turning a hobby into a source of income. Perhaps you love baking – why not sell your exquisite pastries at local farmers markets or set up an online store? Maybe you have a knack for photography – you could offer your services for weddings, corporate events, or family portraits.

But it doesn't stop at hobbies. A side business could also involve offering professional services based on your skills or experience. For instance, if you're a talented writer, you could start a freelance copywriting or editing service. If you're an accountant by day, why not offer your expertise to small businesses or individuals as a side gig?

Then there are side businesses that can fill a gap in your community. For instance, if you live in an area where access to fresh produce is limited, starting a small-scale local delivery service for fresh fruits and vegetables could be a viable business and a way of contributing to your community.

Of course, managing a side business does come with its set of challenges. Balancing a full-time job, a side business, and personal commitments can be demanding. It requires excellent time management skills, dedication, and persistence. Plus, there are practical considerations such as financing, business licensing, and tax implications to consider.

In the following chapters, we will provide a roadmap for starting and managing a side business, exploring strategies for balancing commitments, finance management, marketing tips, and more. As we navigate this path together, you'll discover that with the right mindset and tools, turning your passion into profit could be your next big adventure.

Chapter 7

Real Estate Investments: One Property at a Time

In our quest for multiple income streams, there's one path that has stood the test of time, seen fortunes made (and sometimes lost), and yet, continues to draw people in with its allure of solid, tangible assets. That path is real estate.

Investing in real estate is one of the oldest forms of income generation, and it remains a powerful tool in wealth creation. Whether it's rental properties, real estate investment trusts (REITs), or house flipping, each avenue presents unique opportunities for profit.

Rental properties are often the first thing that comes to mind when we think of real estate investments. The concept is simple: you purchase a property and rent it out. The rent you receive generates a steady stream of income, often enough to cover your mortgage payments, maintenance costs, and still leave some cash in your pocket.

If becoming a landlord seems daunting, REITs could be a more hands-off alternative. REITs are companies that own, operate, or finance income-generating real estate. By investing in a REIT, you get the chance to profit from real estate without having to buy or manage properties yourself.

For those who love a good transformation, house flipping might be your calling. This involves buying a property at a low price, often because it needs significant work, renovating it, and then selling it for a profit. It can be a rewarding process, both financially and creatively.

However, real estate is not a guaranteed ticket to wealth. It's a market that can be influenced by numerous factors, from economic cycles to changes in neighborhood demographics. Managing rental properties can sometimes be a hassle, dealing with tenants and maintenance issues. House flipping requires a keen eye for potential, a good understanding of renovation costs, and often, a considerable tolerance for risk.

In the chapters to come, we will delve into the intricacies of each of these investment strategies. We'll look at how to choose profitable properties, managing risks, securing financing, and navigating the ever-changing real estate market. As you'll discover, with careful planning and strategic decisions, real estate can offer an exciting and potentially profitable route to diversifying your income.

Chapter 8

Peer-to-Peer Lending: The Rise of Social Finance

Money lending, in one form or another, has been around for centuries. From old-time moneylenders to modern banks and credit institutions, the concept of borrowing and lending money is well entrenched in our financial systems. But with the advent of the internet, a new player has entered the stage - Peer-to-Peer (P2P) lending.

P2P lending, sometimes known as crowdlending, is a method of debt financing that allows individuals to borrow and lend money without the use of an official financial institution as an intermediary. The absence of a middleman often means that borrowers can get access to funds at lower interest rates, while lenders can potentially earn higher returns than traditional savings and investment products.

The process is usually facilitated through online platforms that match borrowers directly with lenders. As a lender, you can either lend money to a specific borrower or spread your investment across multiple loans (known as diversification) to reduce risk. The interest rate you earn depends on factors like the borrower's credit rating and the term of the loan.

Some popular P2P lending platforms include Prosper, LendingClub, and Funding Circle, each with its own unique lending criteria, interest rates, and risk management protocols. These platforms generally make their money by charging fees to borrowers and taking a percentage of the interest earned by lenders.

P2P lending can be an attractive source of passive income; however, there are inherent risks involved with P2P loans unlike bank deposits which are insured against default by defaulting borrowers and potential defaulters on repayment of loans by investors. Furthermore, it's an emerging industry and can be subject to regulatory changes at any given time.

But don't let these risks deter you. Armed with the right knowledge and strategies, P2P lending can be a profitable addition to your multiple income streams. In the upcoming chapters, we'll dive deeper into the world of P2P lending, exploring the ins and outs of this innovative form of social finance, guiding you on how to select a reliable platform, evaluate potential borrowers, and manage your lending portfolio to maximize returns and minimize risks. As you'll find out, being a lender could be easier - and more rewarding - than you think.

Chapter 9

Navigating Challenges and Risks: The Realities of Multiple Income Streams

So far, we've discussed various avenues for diversifying income sources and creating multiple streams. Each option, from real estate investment to online entrepreneurship, brings its own set of benefits - offering potential profits as well as providing diversification. But to focus solely on opportunities without acknowledging associated challenges and risks would be misleading.

As with any form of income generation, multiple income streams come with their share of hurdles. Balancing multiple commitments, managing risk, navigating legal and tax implications, and dealing with unexpected setbacks can all be challenging aspects of this journey.

One of the first challenges you might encounter is time management. Juggling a full-time job, a side business, investments, and personal life is not easy. It requires a level of discipline and organization that many of us are not used to. It's essential to set clear goals, prioritize tasks, and perhaps most importantly, maintain a healthy work-life balance.

Risk management is another crucial aspect. Whether it's the risk of a borrower defaulting in P2P lending, a sudden drop in the stock market, or a business idea that doesn't pan out, it's inevitable that you will face some level of risk. The key to managing risk lies in understanding the nature of the risk, diversifying your income streams, and being prepared for different outcomes.

The legal and tax implications of multiple income streams can also be complex. Different types of income can have different tax treatments, and certain business ventures may require specific licenses or permits. It's essential to understand these implications upfront, and where necessary, seek advice from a legal or tax professional.

Lastly, you should be prepared for setbacks. Things may not always go according to plan. A stock you invested in might plummet, a business venture might fail, or a global pandemic might disrupt the economy. Setbacks can be disheartening, but they are also an opportunity to learn and grow.

Though multi-income streams present challenges, their pursuit can be immensely satisfying. From financial security and new opportunities to personal fulfillment and personal growth. We will examine these obstacles more closely in subsequent chapters while offering strategies, tips, and advice that will assist your journey of creating multiple income streams.

Chapter 10

The Dawn of a New Era: Future Trends in Income Generation

In our journey through this book, we've wandered through the myriad of ways to create multiple income streams. We've explored the well-trodden paths of real estate and stock investments, dabbled in the world of peer-to-peer lending, and even braved the wild frontier of digital entrepreneurship. As our journey progresses, let's pause and take a moment to look towards the horizon, pondering what lies ahead. What does the future of income generation hold for us?

One term you've probably heard being tossed around more and more is the "gig economy". This concept, which refers to a marketplace teeming with short-term contracts or freelance work, is like a breath of fresh air sweeping through traditional employment norms. With platforms like Uber for rides, Airbnb for accommodation, and Fiverr for a wide range of services, people have begun to monetize almost anything – their cars, homes, even their skills and free time. As the gig economy continues to blossom, who knows what novel opportunities will spring up in the future?

A more mystifying realm emerging on the horizon is that of cryptocurrency and blockchain technology. For some, these terms might sound like alien jargon. However, the alien is becoming the neighbor very quickly. Beyond being a new form of investment, cryptocurrency opens up novel ways to earn income, such as "crypto mining" and "staking". Meanwhile, blockchain platforms are shaking up finance in ways we're only beginning to grasp.

Automation and artificial intelligence (AI) are another pair of buzzwords that are changing the way we think about work and income. Sure, they might seem like the villains in a science fiction story, threatening to replace us all with robots. But in reality, they're also heroes of a sort, creating new opportunities for income. From teaching AI how to think to designing smart systems, the possibilities are mind-boggling.

Increasingly, the world is also waking up to the importance of sustainability and social responsibility. Investors are no longer just asking about returns; they're also asking about the impact of their investments on the planet and society. This change is giving birth to a whole new breed of investments and businesses that marry profit with purpose.

Finally, who can ignore the explosive growth of personal branding and influencer culture? With the rise of social media, anyone with a knack for content creation and a bit of charisma can build an audience and monetize their influence. From YouTubers to Instagram influencers, it's a whole new world of earning potential out there.

As we venture into these exciting new territories, it's crucial to remember that they also come with their own set of challenges. From navigating regulatory uncertainties to managing privacy concerns and coping with the volatility of new markets, there's a lot to learn and adapt to.

In the upcoming chapters, we'll take a closer look at these emerging trends. We'll demystify them, delve into their potential and pitfalls, and guide you on how you can ride these waves to expand your income streams. So, buckle up and get ready. The future of income generation is here, and it's a thrilling ride!

Conclusion

The End of a Chapter, The Start of a Journey

And here we are, at the end of our adventure together. We've navigated the twists and turns of multiple income streams, diving deep into a sea of opportunities from the familiar world of real estate and stock market investments to the exhilarating new territories of online businesses, peer-to-peer lending, and even the perplexing labyrinth of cryptocurrencies. We've peeked into the future, imagining what our financial world might look like as we steer towards the dawn of a new era.

Through our journey, I hope that it has illuminated for you that multiple income streams aren't just an abstract pursuit for wealth; they represent your journey toward financial independence and equipping yourself with tools to weather life's storms - plus creating an enduring legacy for future generations!

But let's not sugarcoat it - this path is far from easy. It's a winding trail filled with challenging climbs, unexpected obstacles, and sometimes, disappointing dead-ends. You'll make mistakes - and that's okay. Mistakes are lessons in disguise, providing valuable wisdom to guide your next steps.

As you set out on your journey, remember to arm yourself with knowledge, approach every decision with careful thought, and don't hesitate to seek help when you need it. Keep your eyes on your destination but be patient, for the road to financial independence is a marathon, not a sprint.

Above all, embrace and enjoy the journey. Savor the thrill of learning, the joy of discovery, and the satisfaction of seeing your efforts bear fruit. Because, at the end of the day, the journey towards multiple income streams is as much about growing as a person as it is about growing your bank balance.

As we part ways and you embark on this exciting venture, remember that this is just the beginning. Each step forward is a step towards greater financial resilience and independence. So, embrace the challenges, celebrate the small wins, and never stop learning. The road ahead is yours to travel, and I wish you nothing but success. Happy journeying!